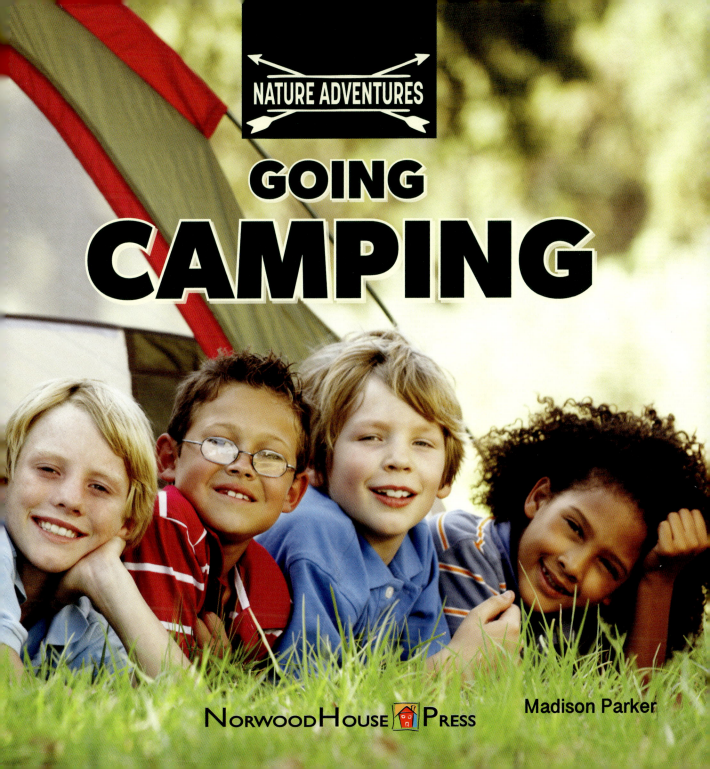

Cataloging-in-Publication Data

Names: Parker, Madison.
Title: Going camping / Madison Parker.
Description: Buffalo, NY : Norwood House Press, 2026. | Series: Nature adventures | Includes glossary and index.
Identifiers: ISBN 9781978574595 (pbk.) | ISBN 9781978574601 (library bound) | ISBN 9781978574618 (ebook)
Subjects: LCSH: Camping--Juvenile literature.
Classification: LCC GV191.7 P375 2026 | DDC 796.54--dc23

Published in 2026 by
Norwood House Press
2544 Clinton Street
Buffalo, NY 14224

Copyright © 2026 Norwood House Press
Designer: Rhea Magaro
Editor: Kim Thompson

Photo credits: Cover, p. 1 Monkey Business Images/Shutterstock.com; p. 5 wavebreakmedia/Shutterstock.com; p. 6 anatoliy_gleb/Shutterstock.com; p. 7 MNStudio/Shutterstock.com; p. 8 ORIONF/Shutterstock.com; p. 9 Olya Humeniuk/Shutterstock.com; p. 11 HildeAnna/Shutterstock.com; p. 12 Chepko Danil Vitalevich/Shutterstock.com; p. 13 Irina Wilhauk/Shutterstock.com; p. 14 B Brown/Shutterstock.com; p. 15 PhotosByLilly/Shutterstock.com; p. 16 anastasiya adamovich/Shutterstock.com; p. 17 Trusova Evgeniya/Shutterstock.com; p. 18 Juice Dash/Shutterstock.com; p. 19 Virrage Images/Shutterstock.com; p. 21 Drazen Zigic/Shutterstock.com

All rights reserved. No part of this book may be reproduced in any form without permission in writing from the publisher, except by a reviewer.

Printed in the United States of America

Some of the images in this book illustrate individuals who are models. The depictions do not imply actual situations or events.

CPSIA compliance information: Batch #CSNHP26: For further information contact Norwood House Press at 1-800-237-9932.

TABLE OF CONTENTS

What Is Camping?...4

Camping Supplies...8

Camping Safety..14

Where to Go Camping 18

Glossary 22

Thinking Questions...23

Index...24

About the Author 24

WHAT IS CAMPING?

Let's go camping! Camping is a fun outdoor activity.

When you camp, you live outside. You sleep outside for at least one night. You are surrounded by nature.

There are many things to do! You can take a hike. You can build a **campfire**. You can look up at the stars.

CAMPING SUPPLIES

You need many supplies for camping. The most important is a tent or other **shelter**. It will protect you from the **elements**.

You will also need a sleeping bag. It will keep you warm all night long.

Fire starters are **essential**. They are made of special materials that burn easily. Fire starters get a fire going quickly.

A fire can warm you up. It can provide heat for cooking. Do not forget to bring food to cook over the fire!

Wear comfortable clothes and shoes. A jacket will keep you warm at night.

Pack a flashlight or a headlamp. It will help you find your way around the **campsite** after the sun goes down.

CAMPING SAFETY

Your camping trip will be more fun if you stay safe. Be **cautious** so no one gets hurt.

An important rule is to Leave No **Trace** (LNT). This means you should not leave trash or anything else behind. Leave the site better than you found it. This protects **wildlife**.

Only an adult should make a campfire. Always stay a safe distance away from the fire. When you are done, **extinguish** the fire completely. This prevents forest fires.

WHERE TO GO CAMPING

There are many places to camp. You can even camp in your own backyard!

Begin by looking at your state's park website. It will help you find campsites near you. Make sure to **reserve** a spot before you go.

Camping costs less than staying in a hotel. It is fun to camp when you travel to new places. Camping helps you explore the great outdoors!

Glossary

campfire (KAMP-fire): a fire lit at the site of a camp for warmth and for cooking

campsite (KAMP-site): a place to set up your tent and other camping supplies

cautious (KAW-shuhs): careful; avoiding danger

elements (EL-uh-muhnts): the weather

essential (i-SEN-shuhl): necessary or very important

extinguish (ik-STING-gwish): to make a fire stop burning

reserve (ri-ZURV): to arrange for something to be kept for you to use later

shelter (SHEL-tur): something like a tent that protects you from the weather

trace (trays): a sign that someone has been in a place; evidence

wildlife (WILDE-life): wild animals living in their natural environment

Thinking Questions

1. What does it mean to go camping?

2. What is the most important camping supply?

3. What should you pack for camping?

4. How can you stay safe around a campfire?

5. How can you find a place to camp?

Index

clothes 12

fire 7, 10, 16

flashlight 13

food 10

places 13, 18, 19

rule 15

sleep 6, 9

sleeping bag 9

tent 8

wildlife 15

About the Author

Madison Parker spent her childhood in the city of Chicago, Illinois. A farm girl at heart, today she lives in Wisconsin with her husband and four children on a small farm with cows, goats, chickens, and two miniature horses named Harley and David. Her favorite dessert is vanilla frozen custard with rainbow sprinkles, even in the winter.